understanding hockey

ISBN-13: 978-1-905540-14-3
ISBN-10: 1-905540-14-0

Author
Julia Hickey

Specialist Consultant
David Whitaker OBE

With thanks to Glyn Sutcliffe (indexer)

Cover photo ©Action Images

Throughout this publication, the use of pronouns he, she, him, her and so on are interchangeable and intended to be inclusive of both male and female hockey players.

Published by

Coachwise 1st4sport

Coachwise 1st4sport
Chelsea Close
Off Amberley Road
Armley
Leeds LS12 4HP
Tel: 0113-231 1310 Fax: 0113-231 9606
Email: enquiries@1st4sport.com
Website: www.1st4sport.com

Produced and designed by **Coachwise Business Solutions**, a brand of **Coachwise** Ltd.
If you wish to publish some material for your organisation, please contact us at
enquiries@coachwisesolutions.co.uk

If you are an author and wish to submit a manuscript for publication, please contact us at
enquiries@1st4sport.com

060072

Contents

Foreword

I am delighted that you have chosen to open *Understanding Hockey* because it means that your interest in the game has been aroused. I hope the contents and structure of this little book will both answer your initial curiosity and encourage you to take your interest further. Like the game itself, the book is fun and has something for everyone.

The clear explanations of the rules and skills ensure that it is informative, while the quizzes, useful tips on diet and training, and the profiles of leading players all contribute to make this a dynamic, interesting and proactive resource. It is put together in a way that allows you to initially explore all areas of this skilful game, while offering plenty of sources for extra information or further study.

I owe hockey a great deal, for it has given me many years of wonderful experience and enjoyment at all levels of the game. It is a game of skill that can be played at whatever level you choose. There is an enormous number of clubs whose intention is to provide competition at the participative level, while others seek to achieve success in the more competitive world of leagues. These two areas also offer the initial route for those players who are motivated to aspire to the very highest levels of international play.

Whatever your ambition, this book can help you in your early exploration and participation. I wish you every success in whatever way you engage in this wonderful game, and hope that you gain as much fulfilment and fun as I have.

David Whitaker OBE
Former England player and Coach to England and Great Britain

Chapter 1

Getting the Most Out of *Understanding* Hockey

There are three possible ways of reading this book. Whichever way you choose, have fun and enjoy the game of hockey.

1 You can read the book from beginning to end. Most chapters are divided into three parts:

- The first part of each chapter provides information that will help you understand an aspect of the game of hockey, whether you want to watch or play the game.
- The second part is a **summary** of the key information about hockey dealt with in that chapter.
- The final part provides **training** tasks to help you check whether you have understood the rules and information covered in the chapter. You will find the answers to these tasks at the back of the book.

2 You can just read a chapter or a section of the book that you think might be useful to you.

- Scan through the book and look for the information (represented by icons) that interests you most. Below is a key to the icons.

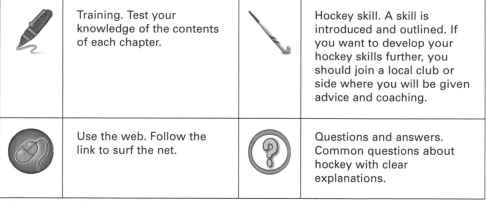

	Training. Test your knowledge of the contents of each chapter.		Hockey skill. A skill is introduced and outlined. If you want to develop your hockey skills further, you should join a local club or side where you will be given advice and coaching.
	Use the web. Follow the link to surf the net.		Questions and answers. Common questions about hockey with clear explanations.

- You can use the summary sections of each chapter to brush up on your understanding.
- You can test your understanding by completing the training activities at the end of each chapter.

3 If you already have some knowledge of hockey, you can also complete the following quiz to find out what aspects of the game you need to sharpen up on. Check the answers (you'll find these at the bottom of the page) to see how well you did and to identify the chapters you should work on.

Quiz

1 What is the maximum number of players a team is allowed to have on the field of play at any one time during a hockey match?
a 12 ☐
b 11 ☐
c 10 ☐

2 Is time stopped for the substitution of players?
a Yes. ☐
b No. All substitutions take place during penalties, the interval and other match stoppages signalled by the umpires. ☐
c Time is only stopped for the substitution of goalkeepers who are wearing full protective clothing. ☐

3 In hockey, what is a bully?
a A bully is a term used by umpires to describe players who use their sticks to intimidate players from the opposing team. ☐
b A bully is a way of starting an international match. ☐
c A bully is a way to restart a match that has been stopped because of injury or where no penalty has been awarded. ☐

4 What penalties can an umpire award, other than playing advantage? (Personal penalties, such as a caution, are not included here.)
a The umpire can award a free hit, a penalty corner or a penalty stroke. ☐
b The umpire can award a free pass, an indirect free pass or a corner. ☐
c The umpire can award a centre pass, a bully or a shot at goal. ☐

5 What is a flick?
a It is an umpire's signal that indicates that a player has been temporarily suspended. ☐
b It is an action where the stick is used to lift the ball into the air. This technique can be used to lift the ball over an opponent's stick, for example. ☐
c It is an action made by the goalkeeper, using his shin pads, to propel the ball away from the goal. ☐

6 What colour cards do umpires use to signal their decisions?
a They do not use cards; they use their whistles and inform offending players verbally. ☐
b Umpires use yellow and red cards to indicate whether a player has been cautioned or sent off. ☐
c They use green, yellow and red cards to indicate whether a player has been warned, temporarily suspended or sent off. ☐

Why not try out the interactive hockey quizzes on the Hockeyweb? Visit www.hockeyweb.co.uk/cgi-bin/quirex/index.cgi

Quiz answers: 1, b (ch4 and ch5); **2,** c (ch4, ch5 and ch6); **3,** c (ch6); **4,** a (ch6); **5,** b (ch6 and ch7); **6,** c (ch8).

Chapter 2

Hockey Through the Ages

The word 'hockey' probably comes from an old French word meaning 'hook' or 'shepherd's crook'. However, a version of the game was played by many, thousands of years before the word 'hockey' was developed.

A 4000-year-old drawing found on the walls of a tomb in the Nile Valley, at Beni Hasan, depicts a game involving a ball and players wielding curved sticks. This image suggests that hockey is a very ancient game indeed. There is also evidence to suggest that the Romans and the Greeks played a form of hockey. Across the Atlantic Ocean, the Aztec Indians may have been playing a similar type of game. Closer to home, there are some similarities between hockey, the Irish game of hurling and the Scottish game of shinty. There is also some pictorial evidence to suggest that a game involving sticks and a ball was played in England during the Middle Ages. A game called hockie was even banned by the Statutes of Galway in 1527 (http://en.wikipedia.org/wiki/field_hockey_history 1 September 2006). However romantic these stories might be, hockey only really began to develop into the game modern players would recognise during the 19th century.

Hockey in the 19th century

At the beginning of the 19th century, public schools began to expand and also to reform the way in which they taught their pupils. The inclusion of many different games in the curriculum was designed, in part, to develop a sense of team spirit and sportsmanship. Hockey was one of the games to benefit from this increased focus on sport, as people began to play it more.

Key Dates

1840 The first recorded hockey club, Blackheath Hockey Club, was established. Only men could join. The first recorded minutes from a club ~~meeting date from 1861 but~~ it is clear that the club was in existence before then.

Find out more about Blackheath Hockey Club's history at www.blackheath.co.uk

1867 *Cassell's Popular Educator* described the game of hockey and noted, in reference to its distinctive hooked stick, that 'No simple rule is laid down as to the form this stick should take'. It went on to say that cricket balls did not survive being hit up and down the field so the best balls to use were 'solid india rubber one(s)' (Howells, 1996).

1875 The first hockey association was set up in England, but it did not survive for very long.

1876 A set of rules was created by a number of London-based clubs. They became known as the Surbiton Rules.

1885 The first clubs in India were set up – the British army had taken the game to India earlier on in the century.

1886	Another hockey association was formed and another set of rules was drawn up, based on those created 10 years previously.
	Slazenger manufactured a spliced hockey stick, which consisted of a piece of wood glued at the bend of the stick. This process allowed the manufacturers to develop a thinner and wider blade than had been possible before.
1887	A hockey club was formed at Molesey.
1894	A women's hockey team from Newham College toured Dublin. The Irish formed their Ladies Hockey Union.
1895	The first ever men's international hockey match took place. However, there is some disagreement as to whether a match held in Rhyl, when Wales played Ireland, or a match in Richmond, between England and Ireland, was played first.
	The Ladies' Hockey Association was set up. It changed its name later to the Women's Hockey Association.

Hockey in the 20th century

Key Dates

1900	The International Rules Board (which later became the Hockey Rules Board) was formed in London.
	To play advantage was recognised as an appropriate umpiring decision.
1901	Hockey was introduced to the USA by Constance Applebee.
1908	The penalty corner was introduced to penalise the defending team when its members committed offences inside the circle.
	The first Olympic hockey competition was held in London and England won the gold medal, while Scotland gained the bronze.
1924	The International Hockey Federation (FIH) was founded in Paris to govern men and women's hockey. This organisation eventually took responsibility for the hockey rules – it ensures that everyone plays by the same ones.
1927	The International Federation of Women's Hockey Associations (IFWHA) was formed.

1928	India entered a team into the hockey competition at the Olympic Games and went on to win all five of its games. Along with Pakistan, India dominated the hockey medal tables for the first half of the 20th century. It was also at this time that the Indian stick grew in popularity. The curve was less pronounced than the one on the English stick. Gradually, the curve was shortened even further, until the stick took the form that it has today. In 1956, the Indian team won the gold medal at the Olympic Games, partly because the players' sticks had a much smaller curve than had ever been seen before and this gave them various advantages.
1959	Umpires were permitted to temporarily suspend offending players.
1966	The FIH gained responsibility for the indoor hockey rules. The game had been developed, and the first set of rules written, during the 1950s.
1971	The Men's Hockey World Cup was played for the first time.
1974	The Women's Hockey World Cup was played for the first time.
1975	The first common rule book for men and women was published.

1976	The hockey competition held at the Montreal Olympics was played on a synthetic surface. Synthetic surfaces became increasingly common during the 1970s.
1979	The green, yellow and red umpire cards were added to the rule book.
1982	The FIH and IFWHA merged.
1986	The England men's team gained the silver medal in the World Cup. They were beaten by Australia, who took gold.
1988	Great Britain's men's team won a gold medal at the Seoul Olympics.
1992	Rolling substitutes were permitted for the first time.
1994	The role of the team captain was developed to make her responsible for team behaviour and substitutions.

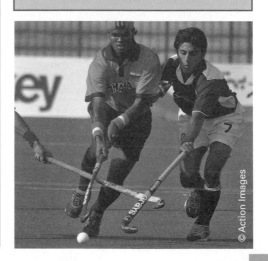

© Action Images

Hockey in the 21st century

Hockey has gone from strength to strength and there are now more than 1000 hockey clubs in England alone.

2003	Reading won the Men's European Club Championships.
2004	The hockey rule book was completely rewritten to make it easier to understand. Some things, such as the penalty corner, were simplified to ensure that the game is as exciting to watch as it is to play.

 To find out more about the rule changes that have occurred over the last 130 years, visit www.fihockey.org and select the 'Rules' from the menu. Then click on 'History of the Rules'. Alternatively, visit www.usfieldhockey.com/history/rules_history.htm for an easy-to-follow timeline of rule changes.

Visit the England (www.englandhockey.co.uk), Scottish (www.scottish-hockey.org.uk) and Welsh (www.welsh-hockey.co.uk) national hockey websites to find out more about the history of hockey in those nations. For a history of Northern Ireland's hockey, visit www.ulsterhockey.com/history/home.htm

To find out more about the development of the hockey stick, visit www.talonhockey.com.au/field_hockey_stick_history.php

Player profile

Dhyan Chand (1905–1979), known as 'the wizard', is considered to be one of the world's greatest hockey players of all time. He was part of the teams that won Olympic gold medals in 1928, 1932 and 1936. When he toured the world with India in 1932, he scored 133 goals but notched up more than 400 goals during his international career. His prowess on the hockey field was so great that, at one point, some players broke his stick to see whether there was a magnet hidden inside it!

 To find out more about Dyhan Chand, visit http://www.bharatiya hockey.org/dhyanchand /aisdara.htm or http://www.planet fieldhockey.com/PFH/Item-View-4635-64

Chapter 3

Getting Started

An impromptu game of hockey can take place anywhere – in the park, the playground or even in your back garden, as long as you have a stick and a ball. The stick is what makes hockey unique and, once the different strokes have been mastered, it is a fast, action-packed game.

 What sort of equipment do I need to have if I want to start playing hockey?

First of all, you will need a hockey stick! You could join a local team or club where you will be able to borrow a stick until you are certain that hockey is the sport for you. Different sticks have different qualities, so it also depends on where you play as to what sort of stick you will require. You will be able to get advice about what kind of stick is best from your coach. Sticks can cost nearly £200 but, as a beginner, you will be able to find one for under £20.

It is also very important to make sure that you wear the correct safety equipment. You should have a gumshield to protect your teeth and gums, as well as shin guards. Some people start off with football shin guards, but hockey ones have more reinforcement and are a good investment if you want to develop your hockey-playing skills.

Players often wear padded gloves and a pair of hockey boots, but these are not essential items of kit for beginners. When you first start playing, you could wear trainers – just ensure that they have plenty of cushioning to protect you as you run, as well as support to enable you to turn quickly. Later, once you have received advice and gained some experience, you may choose to wear a pair of specialist boots. It is also useful to have your own ball, so that you can practise at home.

 **How old do I have to be to start playing hockey?**

You can start playing mini-hockey when you are seven years old; some clubs may accept even younger players. The game is played on a half-sized pitch and each team fields seven players. There are some other amendments to the rules of hockey to ensure that young players learn essential hockey skills and have fun in a safe environment – you can find out about these from Northern Ireland Hockey. There is a national mini-hockey competition run by England Hockey and, in Wales, you can get to grips with the game through Dragon Sport. Scotland and Northern Ireland also play mini-hockey. If you are aged 11–14, you might be interested in England Hockey's Stix Skills Awards. There are four different levels to achieve, so you can keep track of how those all-important stick skills are progressing.

Find out more about Dragon Sports by going to www.dragonsport.co.uk/cgi-bin/dragonsport/baseweb2.exe or check out some of the rules for mini-hockey at www.ulsterhockey.com/youth/mini_rules.htm

If you're interested in the Stix Skills Awards, visit the England Hockey website. Select 'Young People' from the menu and then 'Stix Skills'.

Player profile
Wearing the number-12 shirt, **Jonty Clarke** has earnt a well-deserved international reputation as a formidable right wing since making his England debut against Belgium in 2003. He was part of the team that gained a bronze medal at the European Nations Cup that year, as well as being in the Reading squad that won gold in the European Club Championships. Jonty is dedicated to the sport and knows how to stay calm in difficult situations, in order to score goals and convert penalties. He currently plays for Reading.

© Action Images

Reading has one of the most successful 1XI sides in the country (1XI stands for 'first eleven', which is a club's best team). Find out more about the club by visiting www.readinghockeyclub.org.uk

Do I need to follow a special diet and be very fit to play hockey?

A successful hockey player needs to have flexibility and muscular endurance, as well as speed, agility, balance, a fast reaction time, power, coordination and cardiovascular fitness. This means that the most talented hockey player in the world will suffer as a result of consuming the wrong kinds of food and drink.

If players consume the wrong food or drink on a regular basis, they will not be able to train as hard, nor play for as long, as they would otherwise. This means that players need lots of carbohydrates to give them energy. Remember to eat a high-carbohydrate meal several hours before a game and to have a carbohydrate snack about an hour before the match starts. Players also need to take care of their muscles, as there is always the risk of injury, so consuming plenty of protein is also important. Carbohydrate, fat and protein are the three main fuels for exercise. How much of each should we consume? Well, that depends on the amount of exercise you do. It is also important to eat the right kinds of foods before and after a match. A post-match recovery snack might include pasta and chicken.

Players can also keep up their level of fitness by being careful about the amount of liquid they drink. Water and sports drinks are the best forms of fluid a hockey player can take onboard during a match or training session. Try not to drink lots of fizzy, sugar-filled drinks. Remember, fluid is lost during matches and training as a result of sweating. If your mouth feels dry and you are feeling hot, the chances are that you will be dehydrated. Drinks should always be consumed before, during and after a training session/match, if possible. There are intervals during matches for players to take on fluid for rehydration – do not waste this opportunity. It is important not to become dehydrated, as this will affect your health and performance.

 Check out some hydration facts at: http://news.bbc.co.uk/sport1/hi/health_and_fitness/4289412.stm

The Welsh Hockey Union has produced a nutrition sheet for players (it can be downloaded from www.welsh-hockey.co.uk/coaching_resources.htm). This site also has an IOC (International Olympic Committee) booklet on nutrition, which is available to download.

It is also important for players to avoid injury. You should always warm up by stretching your muscles and joints before beginning a game or a training session. This helps you to improve your flexibility and prevents you from straining any muscles. The stretching exercises should be dynamic rather than static. It is also important to do some cool-down exercises after the game or training session has finished.

If you are just starting out in your hockey career, it is important to eat and train sensibly. The best thing to do is to join a local team or club, where you will receive coaching on playing skills, advice about the sort of exercise programme you should be following and guidance on your diet.

 What do I need to know if I want to start playing or watching hockey?

You need to know the basics first: the field of play, the players, the length of a match, who the match officials are and the scoring system. These are all explained in the rules of the game.

Remember that having the right attitude is just as important as having the correct equipment and knowing the rules; hockey is about respecting the game and each other. The rules also emphasise that everyone involved in hockey must play safely and 'act responsibly at all times'. Treat other people in the way you would like to be treated and play to the best of your ability.

Here are some guidelines on acting within the spirit of the game:

- Thank players and officials involved in the match at the end of the game.
- Remember that there is no room for negative behaviour in hockey. Do not criticise the way someone (either on your own team or the opposing team) is playing. Everyone is doing their best. Always show respect for your colleagues and your opponents.
- Do not be rude or violent.
- Do not use your stick in a dangerous way.
- Remember that players must respect the decisions of the umpires.

Hockey should be about everyone enjoying themselves.

Summary

1 Hockey can be enjoyed at many different levels by players of all ages and abilities.
2 There are modified versions of hockey for younger players, such as mini-hockey, to help them develop those all-important skills and to promote having lots of fun.
3 Join a school team or local side to receive coaching.
4 A healthy diet and sensible training programme are important if you want to develop your skills as a hockey player. The best place to receive this advice is from a qualified coach.
5 The rules are all about playing fairly and safely.
6 Hockey should be fun for everybody.

Training

A Keep a food diary for a week. Write down everything that you eat and drink. Make sure you are eating at least five portions of fruit and vegetables a day.

B Start to think about your level of fitness. Build up your muscles and develop your fitness gradually, otherwise you risk injuring yourself. The best way to get fit is to join a local team. Here is a website that can help you to start finding out about what you need to do to get fit.

   http://news.bbc.co.uk/sport1/hi/health_and_fitness/default.stm

C Find out which is your local team. Some of the information provided in Chapter 10 will help you do this.

Chapter 4

The Basics

All about...a match

Hockey, or field hockey (as it is sometimes called), is played by two teams of 11 players each. Usually, men play against men and women against women but sometimes you find mixed teams, where men and women play together on the same side. Each team tries to score as many goals as possible by using their hockey sticks to hit, dribble or push a small, hard ball into the goal. The opposing team's goalkeeper tries to prevent this. At the end of the match, the team that has scored most goals wins the game. The match is split into two halves; adults play 35 minutes each half, while matches for young players are shorter.

All about...the rules

- The International Federation of Hockey (FIH) is responsible for maintaining the rules of hockey. They make sure that the game is fair and exciting to watch, as well as to play.
- The rules for hockey are the same, whether players are amateur or professional.
- Hockey rules are divided into three sections: playing the game, umpiring and, finally, field and field equipment specifications. In total, there are 22 separate rules. These are then divided into subsections.
- There are separate rules for indoor hockey, although they are very similar to the rules for outdoor hockey. There is also another version of the game called 'zone hockey', which is ideal for players with special needs and disabilities because they can play on an equal footing with able-bodied players. This five-aside game, which can be played indoors or outside, is also fast-moving and action-packed.

 Find out more about rule modifications for indoor hockey at www.englandhockey.co.uk by selecting 'Downloads' from the menu, followed by 'Rules and Regulations'. You can download the rules for outdoor hockey here too.

 If you're interested in finding out more about zone hockey, check out www.ntu.ac.uk/adapted_sports/Zone%20Hockey/index.html – the game was developed by Nottingham Trent University.

The rules

Playing the game

Rule 1 describes how big the pitch or 'field of play' should be and the different features, including the centre line, 23-m lines, circles and penalty spots that should be marked on the pitch. This rule also explains where the goals and flag-posts should be positioned.

Rule 2 explains that there can be a maximum of 11 people on each team on the field and that a team can decide whether they want to have a goalkeeper with goalkeeping privileges or not. It also explains the process for making substitutions and explains that there are no limits to the number of substitutions that can be made.

Rule 3 explains the role of a team captain.

Rule 4 describes what players must wear and the different safety equipment that they should use for their own protection. It also has subsections describing what a hockey stick and ball must be like. There is more information about the stick and the ball in the specification section of the rules.

Rule 5 describes the length of a match, the half-time interval and the fact that the team that scores the most goals wins the match.

Rule 6 explains how to start and restart a match, ensuring that the direction of play changes at half-time. It explains when a centre pass must be taken and how it should be taken. It also explains what a 'bully' is and describes how it should be used to restart a match when play has been stopped for injury or any other reason where a penalty is not awarded. The final section of this rule describes a free hit and when it should be awarded.

Rule 7 describes how play is restarted if the ball goes outside the field of play. The ball must have completely passed over the lines marking the perimeter of the field of play for this rule to be applied.

Rule 8 explains how a goal is scored.

Rule 9 explains the code of conduct that players are expected to abide by and points out that they are expected to play in a responsible way at all times, ensuring fair play and the safety of everyone involved in the match. There is more about the code of conduct in Chapter 3.

Rule 10 explains how goalkeepers are expected to dress and behave during a match.

Rule 11 explains that there are two umpires who control a match. This rule describes the way in which they should use their whistles to communicate their decisions and to let players and spectators know what stage the match has reached.

Rule 12 describes the different kinds of penalties that may be awarded during a hockey match and when they should be used. The penalties include a free hit, a penalty corner and a penalty stroke. The umpires may also play advantage if they think that awarding a penalty against an

offending team would disadvantage the team that was offended against.

Rule 13 explains the procedures for taking the different penalties.

Rule 14 describes personal penalties that the umpires can give if players commit any offences. This may be in the form of a verbal cautioning, a warning (shown using a green card), a temporary suspension (indicated by a yellow card) or a red card (which means that the player has been permanently suspended from the match).

Umpiring

© Action Images/Reuters

Rule 1 explains the ways in which umpires control the game by ensuring that they are knowledgeable, focused, prepared, approachable, fair and consistent in the decisions that they reach.

Rule 2 explains the ways in which the umpires must apply the rules to ensure fair play and minimum interruption to the natural flow of the game. This includes being able to play advantage, making prompt decisions and giving cautions without stopping the match.

Rule 3 describes the skills that an umpire needs and the levels of preparation that are necessary to umpire a match. It also includes an outline of the personal communication and teamwork skills that an umpire requires in order to be successful. The rule explains where umpires should position themselves and the importance of clear communication through the correct use of the whistle and official signals.

Rule 4 describes the signals that umpires use to communicate the different stages of the match, as well as their decisions. You will find many of these signals illustrated throughout *Understanding Hockey*.

Field and field equipment specifications

Rule 1 describes in detail the field of play, its markings and dimensions. It describes how the goalposts, sideboards, backboards and nets should be constructed and what they should look like. This rule also explains what the flag posts should be like.

Rule 2 illustrates and describes the standards that a hockey stick should meet.

Rule 3 describes the ball, its dimensions and its weight in more detail than Rule 4 of *Playing the Game*.

Rule 4 Provides more information about the goalkeeper's equipment.

All about...the different organisations involved with hockey

There are several organisations involved with hockey. These organisations are called 'governing bodies'. They are responsible for regulating, promoting and organising tournaments, leagues and many competitions for various age groups.

© Action Images/Reuters

Table 1: The various hockey organisations

Organisation	Role	Website
International Federation of Hockey (FIH)	This is the governing body for world hockey. It is responsible for developing and supporting hockey around the world, as well as maintaining the rules of the game. It organises both the men's and the women's Hockey World Cup.	www.fihockey.org
European Hockey Federation (EHF)	The EHF is the governing body responsible for promoting and developing hockey within Europe.	www.eurohockey.org
England Hockey	This is the governing body for hockey in England. It is responsible for the development and support of hockey from grassroots to elite levels.	www.englandhockey.co.uk
Hockey Ireland	This is the governing body for hockey in the Republic of Ireland. Northern Irish hockey is administered by Hockey Ireland. The principle office for Northern Ireland is in Ulster.	www.hockey.ie www.ulsterhockey.com
Hockey Scotland	This is the governing body for hockey in Scotland.	www.scottish-hockey.org.uk
Welsh Hockey Union	This is the governing body for hockey in Wales.	www.welsh-hockey.co.uk

All about...the world rankings

National men's and women's teams are ranked separately according to how they perform during a four-year cycle of tournaments. The tournaments that offer ranking points are the Olympic Games, the Hockey World Cup and the Continental Federation Championships. Points are also gained from competing in the qualifying events and are further given to teams competing in the Champions Trophy and the Champions Challenge, depending on their final placement.

Points are awarded based on the team's final ranking in each tournament, rather than on the results of each game. For example, the team that wins the gold medal for hockey at the Olympic Games receives 1000 points. There are 800 points on offer for silver and 750 points for bronze. Points continue to be awarded down to the team who came 30th – they receive 20 points towards their world-ranking position.

 Find out how your favourite country is placed in the world rankings by visiting the FIH website (www.fihockey.org) and selecting 'World Rankings'.

All about...hockey in England and Wales

Hockey in this country is not a professional sport but elite players or athletes, as they are called, can obtain funding. This allows them to work part-time so that they can be fully committed to developing their hockey skills.

Elite athletes from 72 of the best clubs in England and Wales play in the English Hockey League (EHL). There are separate leagues for men and for women. The other national leagues have similar structures to the English one. If you want to find out more information, visit your home country's national website.

Premier Division

Division One

North of England league

South of England league

Five regional leagues   Each region has four divisions within it

The Premier Division contains the top teams in the country. Teams in the EHL Premiership Division can compete for the Super Cup. The winners of this tournament gain a place in the European Club Championships.

The regional leagues are split into five further regions and they are split into four divisions; the ability of each team determines which division they belong to. There are premier divisions and divisions one to three (although the third division may have a different name, depending on the region) and some regions have a **Conference of Feeder** division. Clubs who have their best (first) teams participating in these leagues are able to compete in the trophy competitions. Clubs with teams competing in lower regional and county-level leagues are eligible to enter the Vase competitions.

There are also national competitions for everyone, from the under 11s to the over 50s. Of the several domestic competitions in this country, one of the most exciting is the Championship Cup, which is competed for by teams with an affiliation to England Hockey. The winners of this competition join the three top teams from the Premier Division to play in the Super Cup for a chance to play in Europe.

The Championship Cup consists of four rounds. The first round is played by non-EHL teams. In the second round, the winners of the first round are joined by teams from EHL North and South regions. The third round brings EHL Division One teams onto the field. The final round sees EHL Premiership sides entering to compete for the cup. In recent years, Reading has won the men's cup on many occasions, while the women's cup has been presented to sides from Hightown, Canterbury, Ipswich, Slough and Clifton.

understanding
hockey

 Find out more about some of the competitions that local, county and regional-based teams in England take part in by visiting www.englandhockey.co.uk and selecting 'Competitions' from the menu. Don't forget to visit the other home nations' websites to find out more about their league structure, too.

Some international competitions

In addition to the Olympic Games and the Commonwealth Games, there are several prestigious tournaments for hockey fans to follow. There are men's, women's and junior events that take place outdoors and indoors.

The Hockey World Cup

Every four years, a number of teams qualify in a preliminary tournament. There is a men's competition and a women's competition, which are held at different times and in different places. The teams are divided into pools and compete in a round-robin series of matches. The top two ranking teams from each pool qualify for the semi-finals, while the remainder in each pool play off for the positions fifth to eighth and ninth to 12th, and so on. The top teams from the qualifying tournament then join those nations who pre-qualified because of their previous success – teams who have competed successfully in other tournaments, such as the Olympic Games, and the reigning continental champions. In the past, between 12 and 14 teams have played in the World Cup. They are divided into two pools and there is a further round-robin competition, after which the top two teams from each pool play one another in the semi-finals. Pakistan, The Netherlands and Germany have all won the men's Hockey World Cup in recent years, while the women's World Cup has been dominated by The Netherlands.

Hockey Europe's Championships

There are several tournaments organised by Hockey Europe, including the European Cup Winners Cup and the European Club Championships. The winners of a country's Premiership division gain a place in both these club competitions. The European Nations Championship tournament is played by national teams but does not take place every year.

 To find out all about the different national and international competitions, visit www.englandhockey.co.uk and select 'Competitions' from the menu.

The National Hockey Centre

The national hockey stadium at Milton Keynes is a good place to watch an exciting game of hockey. The centre is also home to the Milton Keynes Dons Football Club. England Hockey is based in Milton Keynes.

www.nationalhockeystadium.co.uk

Summary

1 Hockey is played at many different levels to suit all ages and abilities.

2 International events include the World Cup and the Olympic Games, where elite teams compete against each other.

3 The home nations governing bodies of hockey are determined to improve the sport's profile.

4 Teams play in leagues at different levels, which vary according to the ability of the clubs and the players. This means that games are interesting to play and to watch.

Training

1 Find out about a league team near where you live.

2 Find out who is playing in your national squad.

3 Use the Internet to find out the following information for the men's and the women's 1XI teams:

a In which EHL teams do the current national squad members compete?

b Who is the current captain of the squad and where does he or she play?

c Who are the current national coach and assistant coach for the men's and the women's squads?

d Where are the next Hockey World Cups to be held?

4 Find out about hockey in some of the countries that have a world-class team. Here are some links to get you started:

www.phf.com.pk
www.planetfieldhockey.com

Chapter 5

The Ingredients of Hockey

This chapter details the essential components required for an official hockey match.

All about...the field of play

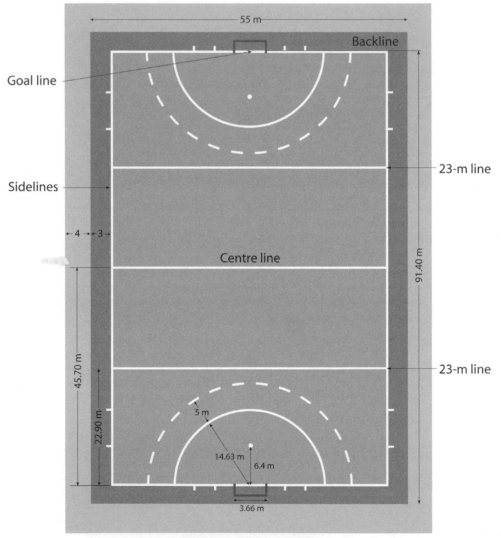

Figure 1: A hockey pitch

The field of play (or 'field' or 'pitch', as it is more often called) is marked out using white lines. These white lines show the boundaries of, and the different areas on, the pitch. They are detailed below:

- The boundaries of the pitch are marked by **backlines** which are 55 m (60 yds) in length and by **sidelines**, which are 91.40-m (100-yds) long.
- The **goal lines** are parts of the backlines that run between the two sets of goalposts.
- The court is divided in half by the **centre line** and there are two **23-m** (25-yd) lines marked across the pitch, 22.90 m (25 yds) from each of the backlines. The area between each 23-m line and backline is called the **23-m area**.
- **Shooting circles** (these are also sometimes called 'striking circles') are semi-circles that extend 14.63 m (16 yds) from the goal at their furthest point. Five metres (5.47 yds) beyond this semi-circle is an outer circle marked by a dashed line.
- **Penalty spots** are marked in front of the centre of each goal. The spots must be 6.4 m from the inner edges of the goal lines. Each spot is 150 mm (6 ins) in diameter.
- The white field markings must not be more than 75-mm (3-ins) wide. This is important because the markings are part of the field of play; as long as the ball is on the line, it is inside the field.
- There should also be additional short-line markings (30 cm/1 ft) outside the field. As these are a more recent addition to the markings on the field of play, they are marked using metric measurements. They are marked 5 m and 10 m from each of the goalposts. There are also lines marked on the sidelines, 5 m from the flagposts, plus another line marked beyond this, which is level with the top of the shooting circle. These markings are

illustrated in Figure 1 on page 18. Older pitches do not have these lines but instead they have lines inside the backlines and sidelines that are the same length (30 cm /1 ft), as the external line markings previously described.

Hockey can be played on different synthetic surfaces, as well as grass. Most top-ranking games now take place on synthetic surfaces. One of the reasons for this is that sand-based or water-based surfaces result in a faster game than those played on grass.

Indoor pitches are smaller and have sideboards around the pitch to keep the ball in play.

All about...the goals

- The two goalposts must be vertical (upright) and must be joined by a crossbar to form a rectangle. The goalposts must not rise above the crossbar and the crossbar must not extend beyond the uprights.
- The goalposts and crossbar should be placed over the centre of the backlines on the external marks, which are each 1.83 m from the centre of the backline.

- The posts must be 2.14-m (7-ft) tall and the crossbar must be 3.66-m (12-ft) wide.
- The posts and crossbar must be white.
- A net is attached behind the rigid frame of the goal mouth. It is fixed into place by back and sideboards, which are at least 46-cm (8-ins) high. The sideboards must be 1.2-m (4-ft) long. The net is loosely fixed to the boards because, if it were rigid, the ball could rebound from the net and potentially hit a player.

All about...the flag posts

The flag posts are:

- placed in each of the four corners of the field
- between 1.20-m and 1.50-m (4–5-ft) high.

All about...the ball

The ball must:

- be spherical
- be made from a material that is hard with a smooth surface. Hockey balls all used to be white but now balls in different colours are used (as long as both teams agree) as they contrast with the different types of surface
- have a circumference of between 224 mm and 235 mm
- weigh between 156 g and 163 g.

What sort of ball should I choose to practise with?

There are lighter hockey balls that can be used by younger players, which are easier to manipulate and strike while retaining the 'feel' of a hockey ball. However, as you grow in confidence and if you are serious about improving your hockey skills, it is a good idea to invest in a proper hockey ball.

All about...the stick

© Alan Edwards

The stick:

- is made up of a handle and a head
- must be smooth
- must have a 'J'- or a 'U'-shaped head. There are slightly different variations to the shapes, and the stick that is used by each player is down to personal preference and to the position played. Players who score goals want a stick with a 'sweet spot' that makes hitting the ball harder and more accurately easier. Other players prefer a stick with a head that is designed for effective dribbling or flicking
- has a flat side and a raked, or bowed, side. The flat side is the playing side of the stick. It is also called the face of the stick. This side of the stick faces the front as you play. It is used to hit and to control the ball
- should not weigh more than 737 g, though the weight is a matter of personal preference and position. Defenders often like heavier sticks, in order to push the ball further down the field
- can be made from anything, apart from metal or metallic parts. It is important that the stick is safe to use and durable. In practice, sticks are either made from wood or a composite material
- can be bound with tapes and resins, as long as it remains smooth and meets all the specifications.

Players can only play the ball with the flat, left-hand side of the stick or with its edges. It is dangerous to play the ball off the raked side of the stick because the player cannot control the direction that the ball will go in. It is also important for players to remember that they should never raise their sticks above shoulder height.

 If you are interested in finding out more about the technical specifications of pitches, sticks and balls, visit www.fihockey.org and choose 'Pitches and equipment' from the main menu.

All about...the teams

- A match is played between two teams.
- There are up to 16 players on a team.
- There may be no more than 11 players from any team on the field of play at any one time.
- There is only one specialist playing position with a defined role – that of the **goalkeeper**. Not all teams choose to have a specialist goalkeeper.
- The other players are called **field players**.
- Each team must decide whether it will play with 10 field players and one goalkeeper or 11 field players and no designated goalkeeper.
- Field players can generally be divided into three groups: attackers, midfielders and defenders, rather like football teams.

Each team must appoint a captain, who then wears an armband to show her position. Captains have a responsibility to organise their team's tactics, to make sure substitutions are carried out correctly and also to ensure that all their players behave in a sporting and fair way throughout the match. If a captain fails in any of these tasks, an umpire can award a personal penalty (see Chapter 9) against her.

Choosing a hockey stick

When you first start playing hockey, you may be able to borrow a stick from your club or school. It is worth trying out a selection of sticks to find out which one feels best for you before you purchase one yourself. Sticks range in price, composition and style. However, it is essential that players choose a stick that is suitable for their height.

Player height	Stick length
Up to 4 ft	28–30 ins
4–4 ft 3 ins	30–32 ins
4 ft 4 ins–4 ft 7 ins	32–34 ins
4 ft 8 ins–5 ft 0 ins	34–35 ins
5 ft 1 ins–5 ft4 ins	35–36 ins
5 ft 5 ins–5 ft 8 ins	36–37 ins
5 ft 9 ins–5 ft 11 ins	37–38 ins
6 ft 0 ins–6 ft 2 ins	38–39 ins
6 ft 3 ins and over	39 ins or more

 This information has been taken from www.pembroke wanderers.ie/sticks.htm

 Visit www.pembroke wanderers.ie/sticks.htm to find out more about choosing a stick.

All about...the players

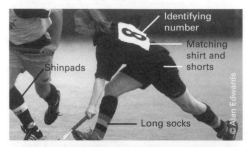

Identifying number

Matching shirt and shorts

Shinpads

Long socks

© Alan Edwards

Gum shield

T-shirt

© Action Images/Reuters

- Players must be able to assume either attacking or defending tactics, but the playing position that a player is given will demand that he is better at some skills than others, depending on the position.
- Players who do not have a goalkeeping role are called field players.

Choosing a pair of hockey boots

Remember that you will need to wear footwear that has a good grip on any surface. Players must not wear spikes – this would be unfair, as well as dangerous, to other players. If you are playing on a synthetic surface, you may choose a special pair of boots called 'turf boots'. If you are playing on an indoor surface, it is important to have a good grip but to not mark the surface of the court. Some hockey matches are played on grass, so remember that you will need a pair of boots that help you gain good purchase – these may be similar to football boots. Hockey players need to be agile and must run quickly, so it is also important that the trainers you choose should be lightweight.

As you become more interested in hockey, your coach will advise you further about suitable footwear. England Hockey recommends that players buy Asics hockey training shoes – see Chapter 3 for more guidance on footwear.

- Players wear a matching kit; women usually wear T-shirts and skirts, while men wear T-shirts and shorts. Players also wear long socks, which cover their shin pads, and specialist hockey boots.
- Players have a number on the back of their shirts, which enables them to be easily identified in the middle of a match.
- Players can wear protective, padded gloves if they wish.
- Players must not wear anything that is dangerous to other players, such as jewellery.
- Players are advised to wear protective shin pads, ankle protection and gumshields. Some associations and tournament organisers require players to wear this safety equipment in order to compete.
- Players are allowed to wear plain, close-fitting face masks if they are defending a penalty corner or a penalty stroke, but only for the time that they are defending the penalty.

All about...the goalkeeper

Helmet

Shirt with number that is a different colour to other players' kit

Gloves

Leg guards

Kickers

©Action Images/Reuters

Teams can decide whether they want a player to be a designated goalkeeper or not. This will affect what they wear.

Option 1 – Designated goalkeeper

- Designated goalkeepers wear kit that identifies them as the goalkeeper. Their shirt must be a different colour to the ones worn by their teammates, the other side and the umpires.
- The goalkeeper's shirt is numbered on both the front and back.
- They wear headgear, leg guards, kickers and gloves. Usually, they also wear chest padding. There are rules about this protection, to ensure that the goalkeeper plays safely and that the game is fair for both teams. For example, the goalkeeper's gloves must not be more than 228-mm wide or 355-m long and the keeper must not have any way of securing his stick to his glove other than by holding it.

- A goalkeeper dressed in full protective clothing may not take part in the game outside the 23-m area.

Option 2 – Designated goalkeeper

Goalkeepers also have the choice of wearing just the shirt that distinguishes them as a goalkeeper plus protective headgear but not the rest of the goalkeeping apparel. If the goalkeeper is wearing protective headgear, she cannot take part in play outside the 23-m area, though, if this is removed, she can move elsewhere on the pitch.

What happens if the goalkeeper removes her headgear?

If the goalkeeper, dressed in a distinctive shirt and wearing headgear rather than full goalkeeping kit, takes off the headgear, she can take part in play everywhere on the pitch.

When must the goalkeeper make sure that she is wearing her protective headgear?

The protective headgear must be worn during penalty corners and penalty strokes.

Option 3 – No designated goalkeeper

Teams can elect to play without a goalkeeper. In this case, all the players wear the same colours and no one wears the goalkeeper's protective gear. If there is a penalty stroke (ie a shot at the goal), one of the field players will be given time to put on a protective face mask to take on the role of goalkeeper.

Teams can change between the three different options when they make a substitution.

I thought that the minimum protection for goalkeepers was a helmet and the foot protectors (kickers)?

Before 2007, teams could use a kicking defender who wore the helmet and feet protectors. On 1 January 2007, the rules described on page 23 came into action.

Why would a team not want a goalkeeper?
It depends on the tactics and the strength of the team. It is important to remember that a goalkeeper in protective clothing may be sitting on the substitutes' bench, so he can be swapped in and out of the game when the captain and the team's manager or coach think it is necessary.

Player profile Carolyn Reid is the number-one goalkeeper for the England Squad and her home team, Bowden Hightown. She's been bringing home international silverware since 1998, when she was part of the team that won the silver medal in the Commonwealth Games. She's taken part in the Sydney Olympics, the World Cup and the European Cup. At home, her domestic honours include a gold medal from the European Cup Winners Cup. When she's not training or playing hockey, she's a school sports coordinator.

© Action Images

All about...substitutions

There are five substitutes on a team. They will be used tactically, depending on the flow of the game.

- There are no rules about the number of substitutions that can be made during a match.
- Substituted players can return to the game, provided that the team never has more than 11 players on the field at any one time.
- Substitutes cannot be brought onto the pitch to replace suspended players.
- Substitutions are made at any time, except between the time a penalty corner is awarded and is finished – the only exception to this is if the goalkeeper is injured or suspended during the corner. The umpire will stop the match to allow the team to replace their goalkeeper. If the keeper has been suspended, the team will have to remove another player from the pitch, in order to bring the substitute goalkeeper onto the pitch.
- Play is not stopped for substitutions, apart from when a goalkeeper wearing full protective clothing is substituted.
- Players must come off and onto the pitch at the halfway line. Goalkeepers can leave and enter the field near the goal they are defending.

All about...the umpires

Every hockey match is overseen by two umpires. The umpires make sure that the match is played fairly and the players need to respect their decisions. It is a very serious offence for a player to disagree or argue with an umpire.

The umpires:

- ensure that the game is played fairly. The spirit of fair play is entrenched within the rules of the game. The two team captains also have a responsibility to ensure that their teams play fairly
- are each responsible for one half of the field. This means that they need to work as a team. They meet to decide their strategy before a match and then communicate closely with one another while play is in progress. The umpire in the half of the pitch where the action is taking place is the controlling umpire. The other umpire moves into a position to support the controlling umpire
- are responsible for ensuring that the match ball meets the specifications set down in the rules and that the players are correctly attired, as well as making sure that the field markings, the goals and the nets are correctly set up
- make sure that the correct time is taken for intervals and each half of play
- start and stop the game by blowing a whistle
- administer the rules and give penalties or free passes when the rules are broken
- keep a written record of goals scored, as well as record players who are cautioned, warned or suspended
- use a number of specified hand signals or whistle blasts to communicate decisions or stages in the match. You will find some of these signals illustrated throughout *Understanding Hockey*.

Umpires need to make sure that they are correctly equipped with an up-to-date copy of the rules, a loud whistle, a stop watch, a pen and a record sheet to record the game. They also need to have a green, a yellow and a red card (used to signal personal penalties to individual players who have infringed upon the rules – see Chapter 9).

In official matches, there will also be other officials (such as scorers and timekeepers) positioned off the field of play. It is the two umpires' job to communicate goals and stoppages, as well as restarts, to the correct person. This is done by using signals.

Umpire profile
David Leiper played international outdoor and indoor hockey in a midfield position for Scotland during the 1980s, making his first appearance on the international stage in 1981 in a match against Poland. In 1996, he umpired his first international game and, since then, he has gone on to umpire many prestigious matches, including the final of the 2002 Champions Trophy, as well as matches at the 2004 Olympic Games in Athens.

 Find out more about some of the umpires who are responsible for ensuring that hockey is played fairly and quickly at many different levels of the game at www.hockeyweb.co.uk/umpires/index.shtml

To find out more about what it takes to become an umpire and some of the qualifications you can gain to help you on your way, visit England Hockey at www.englandhockey.co.uk and select 'Umpiring' from the main menu. Alternatively, go to the National Programme Umpiring Association at http://ccgi.npua.co.uk/Interactive/index.php and follow the links to find an umpires' association near you.

What qualities do I need if I want to become an umpire?

You need to know the game, know the rules and be in control at all times. You should be focused on what you are doing and be fair at all times. You should also be confident to play the advantage rule. A successful umpire must also be able to allow the game to be exciting for the players and the spectators, without disadvantaging a side that has been infringed against. You need good communication skills and you need to be approachable, which helps everyone enjoy the game. Really good umpires strive to improve their umpiring each time they take to the field.

All about...the length of a match

- A match lasts for 70 minutes (1 hr 10 mins).
- It is divided into two halves of 35 minutes each. The teams change ends after the first half.
- The half-time interval is five-minutes long.

All about...winning

© Action Images/Reuters

Each goal is worth one point and the side with the most goals wins the game. Any player, except a goalkeeper in full kit, can score a field goal, as long as:

- the player is within the circle when he hits the ball
- the ball does not go out of the circle between being hit and entering the goal
- the ball passes completely over the goal line and under the crossbar.

What happens if a defender knocks the ball into his own goal?

There is no such thing as an own goal in hockey, so no points will be scored by the attacking team. However, if an attacking player has hit the ball while inside the circle and it deflects from a defender's stick into the goal, a goal is scored. The umpire must follow the ball at all times to know whether to award a goal or not!

Summary

1 There are two teams. Each team has a maximum of 11 players on the field at any one time and five substitutes that can be used throughout the match.
2 The team can have 11 field players and no goalkeeper or 10 field players and a goalkeeper.
3 If there is a designated goalkeeper, she must wear a shirt that identifies her as the goalkeeper. The goalkeeper can wear full protective gear or just the head gear. The team can change the type of goalkeeper they are using through substitution.
4 There are two umpires who work together to ensure that the game is played fairly, flows smoothly and is an exciting sport to watch, as well as to play.
5 Matches last for an hour and 10 minutes. The time is split into halves with a five-minute interval in between each half.
6 The team that scores the most goals wins the game.

Training

A Here is a partially completed plan of a hockey field. Label the different markings and areas on the field.

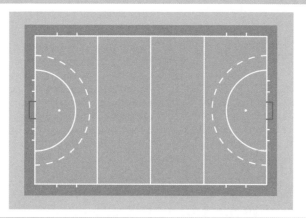

B Look at these statements about hockey. Decide if they are true or false.

i   There is one umpire who controls a game of hockey.

ii The substitutes must not come onto the pitch until the substituted player leaves the pitch.

iii All substitutes and substituted players must come onto and off the pitch next to the goal they are defending.

iv Teams can choose whether they have a goalkeeper in full kit, a goalkeeper with head protection or no goalkeeper at all.

v   Modern hockey sticks are made with an inner-metal core.

vi There is no such thing as an own goal.

vii Goals can be scored from anywhere on the pitch.

viii Only designated players can score goals.

C Watch a hockey match.

i   Identify the different features on the pitch.

ii Note down the different umpire signals you see being used.

iii Look at the way in which players are substituted. When do substitutions occur? Why do you think they are made?

Chapter 6
Following the Progress of a Match

Starting a match

Before the match, a coin is tossed. The winner either decides which goal they wish to attack first or takes the first centre pass, which starts the game.

↓

The umpire blows his whistle to start the match.

↓

All the players, except for the player taking the centre pass, must be in their own defending half of the pitch. Players must be a minimum distance of five metres from the player with the ball. Before the player can take the centre pass, the ball must be still and in the centre of the pitch. The ball can then be hit in any direction, apart from upwards.

↓

The player who takes the centre pass must not play or touch the ball again until it has been played or touched by another player.

When the match restarts, after the half-time interval, the teams will change ends. The centre pass to restart the game will be taken by the team that did not have the centre pass at the previous start/restart of the match.

What happens if the ball lifts into the air when the player takes the centre pass?

It depends on how high the ball lifts into the air. If it lifts less than 20 cm, the umpire will play advantage and allow the game to continue.

Playing the game

The aim is for the players to get the ball into the shooting circle (which surrounds the goal) that they are attacking so they can take a shot at the goal.

As soon as the ball is in play, the players play the ball with the face of their sticks (the flat side) to move the ball around the field. They can hit, scoop, flick or push the ball in any direction they wish. In open play, the ball can be raised to any height, as long as it is not raised through a hitting action and is not dangerous to other players. For more information about a raised ball, read Chapter 8.

Defenders try to take control of the ball, either by intercepting it or by tackling the player who has it in possession. Hockey is a non-contact sport, so a tackler must not touch his opponent or his opponent's stick before playing the ball. As soon as the defending team has possession of the ball, they become the attacking team.

Marking is an important skill for defenders to master. By positioning yourself in the best place, you can either effectively prevent your opponent from receiving a pass or, when they do receive a pass, you can tackle them and gain possession of the ball.

Defenders need to learn how to tackle their opponents effectively. The best place to learn is at school or at a club where you will receive coaching. Why not visit this website to get you started:
http://news.bbc.co.uk/sport1/hi/other_sports/hockey/4186996.stm

Field players must not touch the ball with anything other than their hockey stick - so no kicking the ball! Only the goalkeeper is allowed to use his feet to try and deflect the ball from the goal he is defending.

Stick work is an important skill to master. Players need to be able to control the ball with their sticks, for instance, when dribbling the ball – when the player runs with the ball, pushing it along with her stick as she goes. To do this, you need to work on your grip and make sure that you are holding your stick correctly – developing the right grip is essential in hockey. The forehand grip enables you to run with the ball, tapping it and keeping close contact with it through your stick as you go. Close your left hand around the top of the stick, so that your thumb and finger nearest to it make a 'V' shape. The back of your left hand should be facing in the same direction as the flat side of the stick. Your thumb should be curled around the handle.

When dribbling, your right hand should be positioned lower down the stick. The lower it is, the more control you will have. Look at the photograph to see the way in which the right hand is holding the stick from the other side to the left hand, so that the hand curls around the raked side of the stick with the thumb around the flat side. If you are just starting out, it is important to make sure that none of your fingers are in danger – lay them flat along the top edge of the stick. Some elite players extend their fingers down the stick to add to the control they have. Remember, the best place to develop your grip is at school or at a club where you will receive coaching and advice.

Find out more about stick work and the skills you will need to beat your opponents at: http://news.bbc.co.uk/sport1/hi/other_sports/hockey/default.stm

There are no designated positions named in hockey, as there are in some other sports. However, some players have responsibilities for, and specialise in, defending or attacking different parts of the pitch to ensure cohesive defensive (such as a sweeper) and attacking play; midfield players are versatile and can adapt their game to suit either attack or defence. It is important to remember that players need to work as a team rather than as individuals. This means that hockey teams need to work in formations. A 4–3–3 formation means that there are four players defending their own goal, three midfield players and three attacking players (who try to score goals). Of course, formations are flexible and can change according to the needs of the team and the situation in which they find themselves. Some teams prefer a more offensive formation; others use a sweeper to move into attack or defence as necessary.

29

The hockey rules are designed to ensure a fast-paced and action-filled game. They are also designed to ensure fair play. Infringements either result in a free hit, if the ball is outside the shooting circle, or a penalty corner, if it is inside the shooting circle. For more serious offences, a penalty stroke will be awarded. A penalty stroke is a direct shot at the goal from the penalty mark. There is more information about penalties and how to take them in Chapter 9. The most important things to remember, though, are that you must play fairly, play safely and not obstruct an opponent. You can read more about obstruction in Chapter 8.

Player profile
Ben Hawes plays for England and also for Amsterdam. The Netherlands is one of the top hockey-playing nations, so he knows all about the importance of defensive play and making powerful long-distance shots in his role as half back. Wearing shirt number 14, Ben made his debut on the international scene in 2002 against Scotland and, since then, he has demonstrated his ability on the pitch – he was part of the team that won the gold medal in the European Club Cup in 2005. This sports star is definitely someone to watch!

Ball out of play

It is inevitable that players will sometimes misjudge the distance they need to hit the ball or will fail to stop it. If it goes completely over the sidelines or the backlines, the ball has gone out of play.

 What happens if the ball is deliberately put out of play over the backline by a defender?

A penalty corner is awarded to the other side. The defender's actions could have prevented a goal from being scored.

 If the goalkeeper sends the ball over the backline, does the umpire still award a penalty corner to the other side?

The umpire has to decide whether the goalkeeper's actions were intentional or not. If she decides the goalkeeper's actions were deliberate, a penalty corner will be awarded.

If the umpire believes it was unintentional, the attacking side will take a hit-in on the sideline from a point 5 m in from the corner flag. There is a mark positioned at right angles to the sidelines to show where hit-ins should be taken.

Following the process of a hit-out or hit-in (a hit-out is taken from the backline; a hit-in is taken from the sideline)

A hit-out is awarded to the team that did not have the last touch of the ball before it went out of play.

The umpire checks that the ball is in the right place. If the ball went over the backline, it is placed opposite the point where it went out and is brought 14.63 m (16 yds) from the line onto the pitch. If the ball went over the sideline, it is placed on the line. The player taking the hit-out from the sideline can be on or off the pitch.

All the opposition players must be 5 m or more away from the ball.

The player taking the hit-out hits or pushes the ball into play. The ball should not be lifted intentionally when it is hit or pushed. It must move at least one metre before a member of the same team as the player who took the hit-out plays it. The player who took the hit-out is not allowed to touch or play the ball again until it has been played or touched by another player.

Top tip: The rules for the procedure at a hit-out are the same as those for a free hit. Make sure you read Chapter 9 to understand all about free hits, so that you understand the process involved in a hit-out as well.

 What happens if the ball is stopped on the line?
The ball is not out of play if it is on the line. Therefore, play continues.

 What happens if the hit-out is taken incorrectly?
It depends on the offence. If the ball was raised slightly but clearly not intentionally, the umpire will allow play to continue. If the player taking the hit-out scooped or flicked the ball, played it for a second time or the ball failed to move one metre before it was played by the same team, a free hit will be awarded to the other side.

The bully

Most people remember that, in hockey, there is a set piece called the bully.

These days, a bully is used to restart a match if:
• the ball has had to be replaced
• play was stopped after an accident or some other incident where no offence was committed
• play was halted after a simultaneous offence by both teams.

What does it mean by 'some other incident'?

Another 'incident' is something over which none of the players have control, such as a dog running onto the part of the pitch where the ball is being played or a flock of geese landing in the shooting circle, for example. More realistically, it could be that the ball has become lodged in a player's clothing. Different rules apply for the goalkeeper.

The process for a bully

The umpire signals for a bully to be taken.

The ball is placed near to its location when play was stopped but not within 15 m of the backline.

One player from each team stands on either side of the ball. The players should be facing one another and the goal that they are defending should be on their right-hand side.

All the other players must be a minimum of 5 m from the ball.

The two players place their sticks on the ground to the right of the ball.

The umpire blows his whistle.

The two players tap the flat faces of their sticks together over the ball.

The players are allowed to play the ball.

 How many times do players tap the flat sides of their sticks together?
Once.

 What happens if one of the players infringes the rules?

For a first infringement, the bully is retaken. For a second infringement, a free hit is awarded to the other side.

**Player profile
Stephan Veen** is a hockey legend. He has scored so many goals for The Netherlands gold-medal winning hockey team that it is no wonder that he was named FIH player of the year in 1998 and 2000. As captain of The Netherlands team at the Sydney Olympic in 2000, he scored the three goals that decided the gold-medal winner, reflecting his skill when it came to leading his country to all the major titles.

© Action Images/Reuters

Read about the thrilling final of the men's hockey tournament at the Sydney Olympics and the role played by Stephan at http://news.bbc.co.uk/sport1/hi/olympics2000/hockey/949964.stm

More about scoring goals

© Action Images/Reuters

Goals can be scored in three different circumstances. This can be:

• during open play. A field goal is scored when, during open play, the attacking team gets the ball inside the shooting circle and then scores a goal

• from a penalty corner. This is a set piece and there are some strict rules about scoring a goal from a penalty corner – see Chapter 9 for more information about penalty corners

• from a penalty stroke. This is another set piece. The goalkeeper defends the goal from one nominated player, who takes her stroke from the penalty mark. The rules for a penalty stroke are described in Chapter 9.

 How can the goalkeeper prevent a goal from being scored?
The goalkeeper must always have her stick in her hand but, unlike other players who are only permitted to touch the ball with their stick, the goalkeeper has far more freedom. The rules say that 'a goalkeeper can use her hands, arms, or any other part of their body to move the ball away but only as part of a goal saving action' (Rule 10.2, 'Hockey Rules', p 24). A goalkeeper must remember that, if she is not defending her goal (playing the ball while outside her defending circle), the same rules apply to her as to other players, so there can be no touching the ball apart from with her stick.

 What happens if a player scores a goal from outside the shooting circle?
The goal is disallowed.

 What happens if both sides score the same number of goals?
In some tournaments, the tie will be permitted to stand. However, some tournaments have a 'golden goal' system. This means that an extra 15 minutes are played (7½ minutes each way). If there is no clear winner after this time, the game could go to a penalty shoot out.

Player profile
Australian legend **Rechelle Hawkes** was part of the women's hockey team that won the gold medal at the Sydney Olympics in 2000. Rechelle became one of an elite group to have won three gold medals at three Olympic Games. She had been making her mark on the international stage since 1987 and was Australia's most capped female hockey player. So, what is her advice for budding players? Enjoy playing!

© Action Images

Find out more about Rechelle and the world-beating Aussies at the Hockey Australia website at www.hockey.org.au

Summary

1 Matches are started and restarted with a centre pass.

2 Teams play in formations, in order to attack and defend their goal.

3 All players must make sure that they know and abide by the rules; if they are infringed, a free hit is awarded to the offended team.

4 Players can move the ball up the pitch by hitting, pushing, scooping or flicking the ball. They can run with the ball by dribbling it or attempt to pass the ball to another player on their team. Players must not kick or handle the ball with anything apart from their hockey sticks.

5 The hit-out is a set piece used to return the ball to play when it has crossed the sidelines or backlines, unless it has been sent over the backline on purpose by a member of the defending team.

6 The bully is a set piece used to restart play in the event of an unforeseen occurrence for which no team is responsible, an accident where no one infringed the rules or an event where both teams infringed the rules simultaneously.

7 There are three ways of scoring a goal: a field goal is scored from open play; a goal can result from a penalty corner and a goal can be scored from a penalty stroke.

8 Hockey is a game of skill, speed and agility. These skills are best mastered at a club, where you will receive coaching and advice.

Training

© Alan Edwards

A i What is happening in the image above?

ii When is this set piece used? Refer to Chapter 6 and the Summary (point 6) if you require any help.

B Look at the diagram to the right.

i Which of the balls labelled A to D are out of play?

ii If a ball has gone out of play unintentionally, how should it be returned to play?

iii If the ball is returned to play from the sideline, must the player taking the set piece:
   a stand on the pitch?
   b stand off the pitch?
   c stand wherever he chooses?

iv How far away should the other players be?

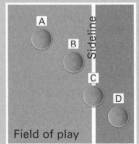

C Watch a hockey match.

i What formations are the teams using?

ii How do the two team captains and their managers/coaches make best use of tactical substitution?

Chapter 7

Attacking and Defending Play

Hockey is about one team hitting, pushing, scooping and flicking the ball along the pitch towards the shooting circle to score goals, while the other team attempts to stop them and score goals themselves. Players attempt to keep the possession of the ball within their team by passing it to one another. Attackers try to feed the ball into the goal circle, so that they can shoot at the goal and score. Defenders try to stop this by intercepting passes and by preventing attacking players from being in a position that is clear of a defender. No player has a restricted playing area, apart from a fully kitted goalkeeper or a goalkeeper wearing protective headgear and a distinguishing shirt. As mentioned in Chapter 6, players play in structured but flexible formations, to ensure they work as a team and have the best chance of winning. Team captains will select or adapt the formation of the team, depending on the circumstances of the game, whether they are winning or losing.

To defend the goal and attempt to shoot goals, players must be aware of the five main types of pass.

Push

Using a quick wrist action with no backswing to move the stick, the ball is pushed and directed along the ground. When the push occurs, both the ball and the head of the stick are on the ground.

Flick

This shot is really an extended push. The player 'snaps' his wrists to lift the ball into the air for a quick pass or shot; in general, however, the ball cannot be raised (see Chapter 8 for further explanation of a raised ball). A penalty could be awarded against you if the umpire believes that you have played dangerously.

Hit

This is probably the most powerful pass in the game. It is used to make the ball travel a long way, for instance, when the defender wants to clear the ball from the shooting circle he is defending or when a player takes a hit-in.

© Alan Edwards

Scoop

The flat blade of the stick is used to scoop the ball up and over the front of an opponent's stick. Players often scoop the ball when they are dodging tackles. To scoop the ball, you put the head of the stick under the ball and then make a lifting movement with the stick.

Slap

This is a hard, quick pass or shot. Players take half a backswing with their hands positioned slightly apart on the stick. It is good for short, accurate shots, such as shots at the goal.

To hit the ball, the player positions his left hand at the top of the stick and brings his right hand up, so that it is in contact with the left hand. This is the only time that a hockey player holding the stick has her hands touching each other.

Attacking play

The attacking team is the one in possession of the ball. Attacking players need to be available to receive passes. This means that they need to get away from defenders who are marking them and denying them the space to receive passes. To do this, they need to be able to 'get free' and move into a space in anticipation of a teammate passing them the ball. Once they have the ball, they need to be able to run with it and avoid being tackled. Attackers play under pressure and have to be careful not to be forced into making a mistake that could result in them losing the ball.

Controlling the ball

Before players can use any dodging or feinting techniques to avoid their opponents, they must be able to control and dribble the ball. Team players also need to be able to pass the ball to one another, in order to advance up the pitch, into the shooting circle.

Watch the video on this website to find out how you could improve your dribbling skills.

While you are there, you can also find out how England performed at the Melbourne Commonwealth Games in 2006. http://news.bbc.co.uk/sport1/hi/commonwealth_games/4827632.stm

Methods of getting 'free'

To free yourself of the opponent who is marking you, you can:

- sprint into a clear, unmarked space
- dodge or leave a marker, by moving one way and then quickly going in another direction
- change pace
- pivot and change direction
- suddenly stop; you can then change direction or, as your marker slows down, sprint off in the same direction as before
- hold a space
- position yourself so that it is difficult for a defender to see both you and your teammate who has possession of the ball.

Top tip: Attackers need to take positive action. It is important to keep moving to stay free of, or to make it difficult for, your marker and to hold space, if necessary, until a teammate is able to pass the ball in your direction.

It is important that the ball is not intercepted when it is passed. This means that players have to pass the ball through an open space to a teammate. They need to be aware of what is happening around them to do this successfully; it is no good just hitting the ball in the general direction of the shooting circle and hoping that a teammate will intercept it before the

© Action Images/Reuters

opposition do. This means that passes need to be accurate. To achieve this, it is important for a player to be well balanced, so that he can pass the ball with direction and force. Once he has passed the ball, he must move into another open space, so that he is available to receive the ball again.

Top tip: Communication is essential. Teams need to be able to communicate through looks and gestures, rather than by words.

**Player profile
Tina Cullen** played as a forward on the England and Great Britain squad, and was part of the team that won the women's gold medal at the European Indoor Championships in 1996 and the silver medal at the Commonwealth Games of 1998. Her domestic honours are almost too many to count but this Hightown player-coach is the National League's record scorer.

© Action Images

Find out about some up-and-coming hockey stars at http://news.bbc.co.uk/sport1/hi/olympics_2004/hockey/3854023.stm

Defending play

Defenders must stop players in possession of the ball and try to win the ball from them. Their aim is to prevent the players on the opposing team from progressing towards and into the goal circle. Once the ball is inside the goal circle, defenders must try to prevent the attackers from gaining a position from which they can take a shot at the goal.

Defenders need to:
- prevent attacking players from gaining space that will be useful for receiving a pass
- gain possession of the ball by intercepting passes or using a legal tackle so that they, in turn, become the attacking team.

Top tip: Defenders need to be alert and they need to move quickly.

Good defenders know a thing or two about tackling their opponents:

- Try to position yourself so that you can see both your opponent and the ball.
- Do not hit your opponent with your stick and do not knock, push or touch your opponent! You will be penalised.

© Action Images/Reuters

Instead, you need to get your stick into contact with the ball when the attacking player isn't in contact with it. If you are far enough ahead, you can position yourself on the right-hand side of the attacker. Then, with your left hand at the top of the stick for greater flexibility, lunge into the area in front of the attacker's stick where the ball is being played and knock it out of the attacker's path, without interfering with the attacker's stick. The important thing is that this jabbing tackle is quick, so that the attacker does not have an opportunity to avoid it.

The most common kind of tackle is probably the block tackle. When making this tackle, the defending player positions herself in front of the attacker so that her right foot is in line with the right foot of her opponent. The defending player must keep both hands on the stick and focus on the ball. When the defender decides to tackle her opponent, she shifts her weight forward onto her left leg and, at the last moment, lowers the stick to ground level to block the ball. The more of the hockey stick that is on the ground, the more blocked the attacker is. If the attacker is running at speed, she will overshoot the ball, which is now being pushed in the opposite direction by the defender's hockey stick.

Defending while inside the shooting circle

The goalkeeper can use any method he wishes to deflect, but not propel, a ball that has been shot at the goal.

He can:

- use his arms, legs or feet to deflect the ball. The important thing to remember is that he must be holding his hockey stick at all times
- handle the ball. No other players can touch the ball unless they are defending themselves against a raised ball that is going to hit their body

- raise his hockey stick above shoulder level to deflect an incoming ball
- lie on the ground to block the entrance to the goal. This is called logging.

The important things to remember are that the ball must not be deliberately deflected over the backline and that only designated goalkeepers can deflect incoming balls, as described above. Any other member of the team defending the goal using anything other than the stick at the correct height will be penalised, and a penalty stroke will be awarded to the opposing team.

 The attacking player has a clearly defined target. The defending player or goalkeeper needs to be in front of the target (ie the goal) and must be watching the ball. Remember that the best place to learn these skills is at a club, where you will receive coaching and advice.

Is a bully awarded if the ball gets caught in the goalkeeper's clothing?

No. A bully is awarded if the ball gets caught in a field player's clothing. In this case, a penalty corner will be awarded.

© Action Images/Reuters

Summary

1 There are attacking and defending phases of play.

2 Teams use structured formations, in order to move the ball up the pitch towards the shooting circle if they are attacking and also to defend their goal from attack.

3 Attacking players must try to create space to receive the ball. They must use their judgement as to where the ball should be passed next, in order to help progress the ball up the pitch so that it can be fed into the shooting circle for a shot at goal.

4 Defending players mark their opponents to prevent them from receiving the ball. They attempt to intercept the ball and to prevent the attacking team from gaining ground.

5 When a defender marks an opponent, he is restricting the attacking player's movements by occupying space and denying him possession of the ball.

6 Defenders try to intercept the ball or tackle attacking players, in order to gain possession of the ball.

7 Players must not touch the sticks or any part of the players from the opposing team. They must not step between the player in possession of the ball and the ball, as this is obstruction.

8 The best place to learn stick control, dribbling, passing, attacking and defensive skills is at a club, where you will receive advice, coaching and plenty of practice as part of a team.

Training

A Watch a hockey match.

   i Take note of the way in which defenders mark attacking players.

   ii Look at the different techniques that attacking players use to get free and move into spaces so that they can gain possession of the ball.

Chapter 8

Obstruction, Dangerous Play, Raised Ball and Other Misconduct

All hockey players must remember their responsibility to play in a sporting and safe manner. This is so important that each team captain has a responsibility for the behaviour of his players. Umpires watch to make sure players behave fairly and award penalties if the rules are broken.

Obstruction

There is no offside rule in hockey but the rules are very clear about where players must stand during set pieces, and also regarding the way that players must behave in open play to avoid blocking their opponents. Hockey is a **non-contact** sport. Players must not touch their opponents on purpose or accidentally. The rules are clear about the need for umpires to make judgements, based on the principles of fair play. This means that players must not tackle an opponent unless they can play the ball without body contact.

Obstruction during open play

Players are committing an obstruction infringement if they:

• back into an opponent
• touch another player or another player's stick
• shield the ball from a fair tackle, either with their bodies or their sticks. This rule is quite difficult for new players to pick up because it is perfectly acceptable to shield the ball while it is being played. The obstruction rule only comes into effect when there is a genuine tackle from an opponent
• shield a teammate who has possession of the ball from a tackle.

The umpire will decide if a player is obstructing an opponent and will signal accordingly, as shown below.

Hockey is a fast-moving game and it is easy to get carried away with the flow of events. In order to avoid the charge of obstruction, players must be in a position to tackle the player with the ball and time their tackle to be in the right position at the best time. The player with the ball could move in any direction, as long as she does not back into her opponent. The best place to learn about and practise tackling skills is at a club where you will receive coaching.

Obstruction by the goalkeeper

Goalkeepers must not lie on the ball.

Keeping the correct distance and not interfering during set pieces

The rules of hockey are about fair play and safety. If an opponent is receiving a raised ball, players must not come within 5 m until the ball has been received, controlled and is on the ground. This is to ensure that there is no risk of injury. Penalties are used to ensure that a team that breaks the rules does not benefit from their infringements. For example, free hits are used to ensure that the team that has been awarded the ball gets a fair chance at keeping possession. Equally, the rules recognise that if a free hit is taken too close to the circle, it would offer an unfair opportunity to the attacking team, from which they could then score a goal.

Free hits

Opponents must be at least 5 m from the player taking the hit. If the hit is within 5 m of the circle and is awarded to the attacking team, all the players, including the hitter's teammates, must be 5 m or more from the player taking the free hit. The dashed outer circle is 5 m from the circle, so there is no excuse for forgetting this rule. The umpire will not always delay a free hit because one or more of the players are within 5 m of the player taking the shot. He will decide whether or not they are influencing play. If, however, he believes that the players are influencing play and that they have repeatedly offended, he could advance the penalty by 10 or he could reverse the hit so that the other team gets a free hit.

Penalty corners

All the players must be outside the circle and at least 5 m from the spot where the corner is to be taken. Only five defenders, including the goalkeeper, are allowed to be behind the backline waiting to defend the corner. All the other defenders must be on the other side of the centre line. You can read more about penalty corners in Chapter 9.

Penalty strokes

With the exception of the player taking the stroke and the player defending the goal, everyone else should be outside the 23-m area. If a player from the defending team comes into the 23-m area and the umpire decides that she has interfered with play by distracting the player taking the stroke, he can order the penalty stroke to be taken again, provided that a goal has not already been scored. If it is a member of the attacking team who interferes with play and a goal is scored, the umpire can order the stroke to be taken again and the first goal does not count. You can read more about penalty strokes in Chapter 9.

If you see the umpire signalling as shown below, make sure that you are at least 5 m from the player taking the penalty.

Dangerous play

Hockey can be an adrenaline-filled game. Despite this, there is no place for rough or dangerous play. When you play, it is important to remember not to intimidate players from the opposing team or to make any physical contact with them. It is also important to remember the rules for using a stick and hitting a ball that were described in Chapter 6. These rules are written for the safety of players. For example:

• players must not use their sticks in a dangerous way. This means that they should not lift their sticks over the heads of other players. If a player uses her stick to tackle an opposing player, the umpire will signal as below

• players should not strike a ball if it is above shoulder height (although it is OK to stop or deflect a shot at goal).

A raised ball

Raised ball

Remember that the rules are there to protect the players. As a raised ball can be dangerous, there are three important things to remember:

• A player, unless he is shooting at the goal, must not intentionally raise the ball when hitting it.

• Balls should not be deliberately raised and targeted at other players.

• A player must not hit a ball that is already travelling at shoulder height! This also includes raising the ball from the ground and then hitting it.

The only players who should attempt to play a ball at, or above, shoulder height are the goalkeepers. They should try to stop the ball or deflect it but should not try to propel it – this would be dangerous.

The umpire signals as shown above when he believes the raised ball is dangerous. Otherwise, he will play advantage where there has been no intention of raising the ball and where there is no danger to other players.

In order to make the ball travel long distances, surely the ball needs to be in the air?

Yes, an aerial ball can be used to send the ball a long distance. The idea is that the player will avoid the opposition by sending the ball over their heads. However, the ball should be scooped rather than hit. It is also important that, when the ball is coming back down to earth, only one player receives it. The other players should retreat 5 m until the ball is controlled and on the ground.

Other misconduct

Players should always remember the respect that is due to everyone involved in the game. If they fail to show the courtesy other players deserve, they will be penalised.

**Player profile
Robert Hammond Oam** made his international debut for the Australian Kookaburras in 2001 and, since then, has demonstrated his skill and versatility as a midfield player. In 2003, he helped his squad gain second place in the Champions trophy and, a year later, he was part of the squad that took the gold medal at the Athens Olympic Games. In 2006, he celebrated a gold medal win at the Melbourne Commonwealth Games. This same year, the Australians were narrowly beaten into second place by the German team, who won 4–3.

Intimidation of any kind is not allowed. The umpire will award a free hit and a personal penalty if he sees this.

A **bad temper** has no place in a hockey match. Violence and abusive language will be severely penalised by the umpires. This includes throwing anything onto the field or at another participant in the match.

Handling or kicking the ball was explained in Chapter 6. Players have a stick to control, hit, push, flick or pass the ball. No player should use her hands or feet – in fact, any part of her body – to control the ball in any way. If the ball accidentally hits a player and is stopped or deflected, it is not an offence. Only the goalkeeper can stop the ball with her hands. If a player is hit because of a raised ball, the player who hit the ball will be penalised for raising the ball dangerously.

What happens if the ball flies through the air towards a player and she stops it with her hands in order to stop it hitting her?

Assuming that the player didn't intentionally run into the path of the ball, the person who hit the ball has played dangerously and will be penalised. Remember that the hockey rules are there to protect fair play.

Players without a hockey stick will be penalised! It is also an offence to throw your stick at anyone or anything.

Time wasters are not playing according to the spirit of the game and should be penalised. If a team is slow to take its free hit, it is perfectly acceptable for the umpire to blow his whistle and reverse the hit, so that the other team takes it. The umpires will ensure that a side does not benefit from delaying tactics.

Summary

1 The hockey rules emphasise and protect fair play and the safety of everyone involved in the match.

2 There is no offside rule but there are clearly defined obstruction rules.

3 Players must make sure that they do not use their sticks dangerously and they must ensure that, if they are engaged in active play, they are using their sticks. Players without sticks are penalised.

4 Players must not deliberately raise the ball from a hit or hit a ball that has already been raised.

5 Aerial balls are permitted, provided they are not hit into the air. One acceptable way of lifting the ball is to scoop it upwards for a long-distance shot but, when the ball lands, players should stay 5 m away from the player receiving the ball, until it has been received, controlled and is on the ground.

6 It is against the rules to intimidate another player.

7 Players must not have any contact with one another, either accidentally or deliberately. The umpire will make his decision based on the actions of both players.

8 It is important for players to remember the rules for set pieces, as these determine how close players can stand to the ball before the hit or stroke is taken and also what area of the pitch players should be standing in.

9 Umpires will award match penalties and personal penalties to players who break the rules of the game.

10 Players should behave within the spirit of the game and respect one another.

Training

A Look at the umpire signals below. Identify the offence that the umpire is signalling has been committed.

	Umpire's signal	Offence
i		
ii		
iii		
iv		
v		

B Watch a hockey match. Do you agree with the umpire's decisions?

Chapter 9

Penalties, Playing Advantage and Other Sanctions

Hockey is a fast-moving game that is based on fair play, as laid out in the Rules of Hockey. Players value one another and their spectators; they also respect the umpires and the decisions that the umpires make during a match.

If an umpire sees an infringement of the rules, she will stop play and signal which penalty is to be taken and where it will be taken from – players must make sure that they follow the umpire's instructions carefully. The penalty can be a match penalty, a personal penalty or both and that which is awarded will depend on the offence and where on the pitch it was committed.

Playing the advantage

The game should flow without too much interruption from the umpires. If an umpire sees an offence that is not creating a disadvantage for the non-offending team, or where stopping the game would cause a disadvantage to the non-offending side, she plays the advantage and the game is allowed to continue.

The umpires need to keep the game under control, though, and will stop the game if a player offends repeatedly or if the decision to play advantage would be unfair to the non-offending side.

 Would it be right to say that the umpire will play advantage if the non-offending side has possession of the ball?

The key thing to remember is that the umpire must feel that the non-offending side will be able to develop its play. If the umpire feels that the non-offending side will suffer as a consequence of the infringement, she may well stop the match and award a penalty, even if the non-offending side has the ball. Umpires have a very important role to play in balancing the pace and action of the game with the need to ensure fair play at all times. This means that the skills of being able to anticipate the flow of the match and be aware of what could happen next are very important for an umpire.

Match penalties

There are three match penalties that an umpire can award: a free hit, a penalty corner and a penalty stroke.

The free hit

Free hits are awarded for basic offences, such as raising a stick too high, obstruction, tackling improperly or kicking the ball. The purpose of awarding this penalty is to ensure that the ball is in the possession of the non-offending team. The umpire can award free hits against attackers anywhere on the pitch; free hits against defenders can also occur anywhere, unless the offence was committed inside their own defending circle.

Remember that you cannot take a shot at the goal from a free hit.

The process of a free hit

If a player obstructs another player, makes contact or moves a goalpost, for instance, it is clearly unfair and to play advantage would be unfair to the non-offending team.

↓

The umpire blows her whistle and signals for a free hit to be taken.

↓

Any player from the non-offending team can take the free hit, as long as they are close to where the offence took place – this is particularly important if the offence took place within the 23-m area. If the free hit has been awarded to the defending players inside their defending circle, the hit may be taken anywhere inside the circle.

↓

The opposing team must be at least 5 m from the ball before the hit is taken. If the hit is taken by an attacking player within 5 m of the circle, all the players (apart from the one taking the free hit) must be 5 m from the ball. To check if this is the case, look to see if the ball is positioned inside the dashed outer circle; if it is, everyone should be 5 m from the ball before it is hit.

The ball must be stationary before it is hit. The player who hits the ball must not intentionally lift it into the air;

instead, the ball should be hit on or near to the surface of the pitch. However, so long as the ball is not dangerous and does not give the team taking the hit an unfair advantage, the umpire is unlikely to penalise the hit.

↓

The ball must travel at least one metre before another player from the same team can touch the ball. The player who took the hit must not hit the ball again until it has been played by another player.

↓

Free hits should be taken as quickly as possible to ensure fair play and a good game. If an umpire believes that a team is deliberately delaying the free hit, she can move the location from which the hit is to be taken by 10 m to advantage the other team.

The procedure for taking a free hit is the same as the procedure for taking a hit-out.

Advancing a free hit by 10 metres

The umpire has the option to move a free hit further up the pitch if she wishes. This is referred to as advancing or progressing the free hit. An umpire may choose to do this if the offending side commits a second offence immediately after the first one. For instance, they may:

- argue about the penalty that has been awarded
- behave in an unsporting manner by trying to delay the penalty from being taken or deliberately failing to move 5 m away from the ball.

 Will the umpire always advance the free hit in these circumstances?

Increasing the penalty is entirely up to the umpire. However, she has to ensure that she administers penalties fairly; she has to be sure that the offences are deliberate, rather than unintentional, and that she applies the same rules to both teams. It is also possible for the umpire to reverse a free hit; the team that originally had the free hit awarded against it, is now directed to take a free hit. The umpire will award this sort of free hit if that original free hit is not taken fairly (for instance, if the player who took the hit failed to hit the ball at least one metre, played the ball for a second time before it has been played by another player or delayed taking the hit until his own players were in the best tactical positions).

Did you know that a free hit cannot be advanced so that it is taken inside the circle? Rather than advance the free hit by 10 m, if the offence has been committed inside the 23-m area by the defending team, the umpire can change the free hit to a penalty corner.

The penalty corner

Penalty corners are awarded against defending teams if they:

- intentionally commit offences in the circle that do not prevent a goal from being scored. This includes offences against players who do not have the ball or an opportunity to play the ball
- unintentionally commit offences in the circle
- commit intentional offences within the 23-m area (25-yd area)
- deliberately play the ball over the backline. Only a goalkeeper can deflect the ball in this direction without being penalised.

Top tip: Umpires will play advantage if they think that it would be unfair to the attacking players by interrupting the flow of the game. This is especially true if the offending defence player has not deliberately infringed the rules.

Defending players wait behind the backline for a penalty corner to be taken

The process for taking a penalty corner

A defending player commits an offence inside the 23-m area or inside the circle. For example, a defending player obstructs an attacking player inside the circle. It is clearly unfair and, to play advantage, would be unfair to the non-offending team.

↓

The umpire blows her whistle and signals that a penalty corner must be taken.

↓

The ball is placed on the backline. It must be at least 10 m from the goalposts and can be either on the right or left of the circle – the players taking the corner can choose which is best for them.

↓

All players, both attacking and defending, must be at least 5 m from the ball when the penalty corner is taken. All of the attacking players, apart from the player nominated to take the corner, must be on the pitch, outside the circle (this applies to the player's sticks, which must also be outside the circle). Up to five defenders, including the goalkeeper if there is one, can be positioned behind the backline. They must remember that the rule of not being inside the circle applies to them just as it applies to the attacking players. They must be careful to have their feet, hands and sticks behind the backline. The rest of the defending players must be positioned beyond the centre line.

The umpire responsible for the other half of the pitch will move into a position to support the controlling umpire.

↓

The player takes the hit or the push. The player must have at least one foot outside the field of play and must not deliberately raise the ball when he hits or pushes it. The player who takes the penalty corner cannot score a goal from his initial hit.

↓

Until the ball has been hit, no attackers or defenders can enter the circle. If the defenders move too early, which would give them an advantage, the umpire will order the penalty corner to be retaken. If the defenders repeatedly infringe the rule, the umpire can award a penalty stroke to the other team.

↓

The player who took the penalty corner must not play the ball or come within playing distance of the ball until it has been played by someone else.

↓

The attacking team cannot score a goal from a penalty corner until the ball has travelled outside the circle.

↓

There are different rules to remember about scoring a goal from a penalty corner:
- For the **first shot at goal**, if the ball is hit (rather than pushed, flicked or scooped) across the goal line, it must not be higher than 460 mm (the same height as the backboard) in order for a goal to be scored. If the first shot at the goal is too high, the umpire will penalise the shot, even if it has deflected off another player's stick before passing over the goal line.

- For **second, third or more shots at goal**, the ball is allowed to be at any height, as long as it is not dangerous.
- If **the ball is flicked or scooped**, it does not matter what height the ball is at when it crosses the goal line, as long as it is not at a height that is dangerous.

The penalty corner is not over until:

- a goal is scored
- the ball travels more than 5 m outside the circle (it goes beyond the dashed outer circle)
- the ball leaves the circle for a second time
- an attacker commits an offence
- a defender commits an offence where a new penalty corner is not awarded
- a penalty stroke is awarded
- the ball is knocked over the backline by an attacker or, unintentionally, by a defender.

 Get some top tips about taking a penalty corner from http://news.bbc.co.uk/sport1 /hi/other_sports/hockey/ default.stm

 Are there any other circumstances where the umpire will award a penalty corner?
If a ball becomes stuck in a defending player's equipment or clothing while they are inside the circle, the umpire will award a penalty corner to restart the game.

 I thought that the penalty corner could be taken anywhere on the backline between the goalpost and the 10-m mark. I also thought that the ball had to be stopped before a first shot could be made at the goal. Have I misunderstood the rules?

No. In the past, the rules for taking a penalty corner were as you described them. The FIH and the people responsible for updating the rules make small changes from time to time to ensure that the game is fair to play, as well as being action-packed. This is why, if you want to play hockey properly, you need to make sure you have an up-to-date copy of the rules.

 What happens if the attackers move before the ball has been hit?
If this happens, the umpire can award a free hit to the defending team.

 What happens if the umpire signals for a penalty corner as the match reaches half-time or its conclusion?
The umpire will allow the match to continue until the penalty corner is completed. This rule also applies if the attacking team is about to take, or is part way through taking, a penalty stroke.

 Is it permitted for the player taking the penalty corner to change his stick before taking the penalty corner?
No, it is not! Sticks have different qualities, depending on their weight and the shape of their head. It would give the player taking the corner an unfair advantage if he was able to swap his stick before taking the corner. The same rule applies to players taking penalty strokes; they are not allowed to swap their stick. Of course, if it has been broken, players are allowed to change the broken stick for a fresh one.

The penalty stroke

Penalty strokes, or penalty flicks as they are sometimes known, are awarded against the defending team if:

- they repeatedly cross the backline into the circle during a penalty corner before the ball has been hit by the player nominated to take the penalty corner
- a player commits an intentional offence inside the circle against an attacker who has possession of the ball
- a defending player commits an offence inside the circle, which probably prevents the attacking team from scoring a goal.

© Action Images/Reuters

The process for taking a penalty stroke

A defending player commits an offence that prevents the attacking team from scoring a goal.

↓

The umpire signals that time and play have been stopped and that a penalty stroke must be taken.

↓

If the defending team has a goalkeeper, the goalkeeper will defend the goal; otherwise, a nominated player defends the goal. The other 10 defenders must be outside the 23-m area and they must not interfere with or distract the attacking player taking the penalty stroke. The other 10 members of the attacking team should also be outside the 23-m area.

The ball is placed on the penalty spot.

↓

The attacking player taking the penalty stroke must be behind the ball and must be within playing distance of the ball before taking the stroke. The goalkeeper or defending player must have both feet on the goal line and must not move from the goal line until the ball is played. If the defending player leaves the goal line or moves either foot before the stroke has been taken, the umpire will warn the player with a green card. If the defending player repeats the offence, he will be suspended and sent off the pitch. In this case, if the team has a fully equipped substitute goalkeeper on the bench, that keeper must take up his position on the goal line – another player has to leave the pitch so that the team is still a player down. If there is no fully equipped keeper on the bench, a field player has to take the place of the defending player. If the defending player infringes the rules and prevents a goal from being scored, then the umpire will award a penalty goal to the other team.

↓

Once the players are in position, the umpire blows his whistle.

↓

The penalty stroke can only be taken once the whistle has been blown. It is important for the player taking the stroke to make the stroke as soon as possible after the whistle has been blown. The rules make it clear that delaying the penalty stroke is not acceptable. The ball should be pushed, flicked or scooped. It does not matter how high the ball comes up from the ground.

↓

The player taking the penalty stroke is only allowed to play the ball once.

The penalty stroke is completed once a goal has been scored, once the goalkeeper has stopped the ball or as soon as the ball leaves the circle.

If a goal has been scored or the umpire awards a penalty goal, the game is restarted with a centre pass. If the goalkeeper stops the ball inside the circle or the attacking player infringes the rules, the umpire will blow his whistle and the game will be restarted with a defensive hit, 4.63 m (16 yds) in front of the centre of the goal line.

What happens if the ball is caught in the goalkeeper's clothing?

If this happens during a penalty stroke, the rules say that the stroke is completed because the goalkeeper or defending player has stopped the ball.

Isn't it dangerous if the defending player is not a goalkeeper and so isn't wearing a goalkeeper's protective clothing?

The rules take the safety of the players very seriously. If the player is a goalkeeper, then he should be wearing protective headgear and, if the player is a field player, he should be wearing a protective face mask.

The penalty stroke is a set piece that requires a specialist player who is able to stay calm and focused under pressure, while taking the shot. The stroke is often called the penalty flick because the flick is often used for shooting at the goal.

The player starts to play the stroke from behind the ball but within playing distance of it. As she takes it, she will take one step forwards. The player's weight starts on her trailing foot, rather than the leading foot. The stick is angled backwards so that the head is behind the ball and can get beneath it for lift. It is also important for players flicking the ball to make sure that they start with their hands spread apart as they hold the stick. The hand furthest down the stick should move up towards the top of the stick as the ball is flicked to help create power. Positioning is a matter of wrist strength and personal preference.

The player then steps forward, so that the leading foot is parallel to the ball and the player's body and stick are lowered; this ensures that there is an upwards momentum behind the ball when it is flicked.

As the stroke is taken, the ball is carried upwards on the stick and flicked forward, as shown in the image below.

© Action Images/Reuters

Player profile Jane Sixsmith MBE is one of the best-known female hockey players ever. She has scored over 100 goals and won 165 caps for England and 158 for Great Britain, for whom she won a bronze at the 1992 Barcelona Olympics. Jane is also the only British female hockey player to have appeared at four Olympic games, including Sydney 2000. Although Jane retired from the international scene in 2005, she still plays hockey at club level for her home town, Sutton Coldfield.

Personal penalties

As well as awarding penalties against an offending team, the umpire can also award a personal penalty. Hockey players are expected to behave according to the spirit of the game, and umpires apply the penalties to players who break the rules and suspend players who repeatedly flaunt the laws or behave in an unfair way. Normally, the umpire will caution and then warn players before suspending them.

The penalties reflect the seriousness of the offence and also the number of times that a player has offended. Personal penalties include:

- a **caution**. This is an informal verbal warning and can be given as soon as possible after the offence has been committed, without the need to stop the match
- a **warning**, which is indicated when the umpire shows a green card
- a **temporary suspension**, which is indicated by a yellow card. Umpires suspend players from the game for five minutes or more. If an offence is serious, such as if a player has been playing dangerously, or it is a repeat suspension, a 10-minute stint in the sin bin is awarded
- a **permanent suspension** from the match that is being played, which is indicated by a red card.

When are warnings given?

Players will be warned if they make an inappropriate comment or behave in a way that is not in keeping with the spirit of the game. This normally means that they have repeatedly broken the rules – intentionally or unintentionally – or have behaved in a way that could be described as rough or dangerous. The nature of the warning or suspension, and the length of time that a player is suspended, reflects the seriousness of the offence.

If a player offends more than once, must the penalties escalate in seriousness?

Umpires can award the same personal penalty to a player, as long as the player's offence is different on each occasion. This means that he can't be given the same card for the same type of offence. Instead, having received a green card the first time he committed the offence, on the second occasion, the player would be issued a yellow card. If the player receives a second yellow card, the length of suspension will be longer. The important thing to remember is that the umpire must award a more serious personal penalty against a player, if he repeats an offence that has already been penalised. The umpire can, and will, issue a red card if a player's behaviour is totally unacceptable, without having issued the other cards beforehand.

Suspending players

If a player is suspended, he is required to leave the pitch for the length of time specified by the umpire. The player's team must compete with one player down until the suspended player is permitted to return to the match.

The process of suspending a player

A player has repeatedly broken the obstruction rule, for example.

↓

The umpire signals for the timekeeper to stop the clock or to 'hold time'.

The umpire tells the player what his offence is and how long he has been suspended for. This should be in proportion to the offence. The player must leave the field and, if it is an official or international match, sit in the sin bin. In the absence of a sin bin, the player may be sent to his team bench.

↓

The umpire tells the timekeeper how long the player has been suspended for and then signals the restart of the clock and the match by blowing his whistle.

↓

The game continues. The offending player's team must play with 10 players (assuming that they started with 11 and that only one player has been suspended).

↓

The player is allowed to return to the game after the period of his suspension.

Can the team reallocate playing roles while the suspended player is off the pitch?

If the suspended player is the captain, another player should already have been designated to take over the role during the time of the suspension. If the goalkeeper is suspended, another fully kitted goalkeeper can be brought on, provided another of the team's players who is on the field is removed.

Can the umpire award a penalty against the offending team and a personal penalty against the player who committed the offence at the same time?
Yes.

Summary

1 The hockey rules are about respecting your fellow players. As long as players respect one another and their spectators, there is little likelihood of anyone behaving unfairly.

2 Umpires use signals and their whistles to communicate with the players.

3 There are three different types of match penalty: free hits, penalty corners and penalty strokes.

4 In addition to match penalties, umpires can award personal penalties against individual players. A player may receive a verbal caution; a warning, indicated by a green card; a temporary suspension, shown by a yellow card; and permanent suspension from the match, shown by a red card. Umpires have discretion as to the way in which personal penalties are awarded, but must not give the same penalty for a repeat offence and must make sure that they are firm in their control of the game. This means that violent offences will result in a red card without any preliminary warnings.

5 The controlling umpire is the umpire who is responsible for the half of the pitch where the offence has been committed. The supporting umpire is the one responsible for the other half of the pitch. The supporting umpire is expected to move into a position where she can help the controlling umpire during set pieces, such as a penalty corner and penalty stroke.

6 Free hits are used on the field of play outside the circles to ensure that the non-offending team has control of the ball.

7 Free hits can be advanced up the pitch by 10 m if the umpire decides that the offending team has re-offended by delaying, obstructing or arguing too much against the penalty. The advance cannot be carried into the circle but the umpire can upgrade the penalty to a penalty corner. Free hits can also be reversed if the team awarded the hit breaks the rules for taking it.

8 Penalty corners and penalty strokes are awarded against the defending team.

9 Penalty corners are awarded for unintentional offences that occur inside the circle but haven't prevented goals from being scored. They are also awarded for intentional offences against players without the ball inside the circle and for intentional offences in the 23-m area.

10 Penalty strokes are awarded against defenders who repeatedly break the rule that requires them not to cross the backline into the circle before a penalty corner has been taken, and for infringements of the rule, both intentionally and unintentionally, inside the circle that prevents a goal from being scored.

11 These penalties are set pieces. The rules explain the procedure for taking each of the penalties. One of the most important elements of each set piece is that players must stay the correct distance away from the ball and the player taking the hit, corner or stroke, until the penalty has been taken.

12 It is important for players involved in set pieces, like the penalty corner, to wait until the whistle is blown before moving, or else a penalty will be awarded against them.

13 It is important to study the rules carefully, as the FIH often makes changes to the rules to improve the game.

14 The umpire can also play advantage where it is clear that the non-offending team would be penalised if the umpire was to stop the match to administer a penalty. It is also important that the flow of the game is maintained, so that it is interesting to watch as well as to play.

15 Umpires can warn, suspend and, ultimately, send players off who repeatedly offend or behave in an unsporting manner.

16 If a player is suspended or sent off the pitch, the remaining team must continue to play one person down. A substitute cannot be brought onto the pitch to continue the game in place of the suspended or dismissed player, unless the suspended player is a goalkeeper or a player in the role of goalkeeper.

In this case, another player from the same team must be removed from the pitch when the fully kitted substitute goalkeeper walks on to the field of play, to ensure the team is still playing one man down. Alternatively, a field player must be given time to put on the appropriate face mask protection.

17 The spirit of the game is very important. Hockey players are expected to play to the best of their ability and in a sporting way.

Training

A What is this signal opposite communicating and when does the umpire use it?

B You are the umpire. Decide what penalty you would award in each of the cases described in the table below.

Offence	Penalty
A player is in the midfield. He has barged into another player, preventing them from gaining possession of the ball.	
A defending player has deliberately knocked the ball across the backline. The player is not the goalkeeper.	
While waiting for a penalty corner to be taken, a defending player positioned behind the backline repeatedly moves into the circle. The umpire has already warned the player.	
Before a penalty stroke has been taken, the goalkeeper moves his feet from the goal line.	

C Watch a hockey match. Note down the ways in which the players and the spectators show their appreciation of good playing.

D Watch another hockey match. Make a note of the way in which the umpires work as a team. How does the supporting umpire assist the controlling umpire?

E Watch a third hockey match. Make a note of the different penalties that are awarded. Can you explain why the umpires make each of their decisions?

Chapter 10

Finding Out More

If you want to find out more about getting involved in hockey, why not join a team – it could be at school or at a local club. England, Ireland (remember, Northern Irish hockey is administered by Ireland Hockey), Scotland and Wales all have governing bodies and organisations committed to developing hockey for young people. England Hockey has five regional academies and five regional development managers who are there to help you find out all you need to know to get involved in the game of hockey.

 If you are interested in finding out about English clubs, go to www.englandhockey.co.uk and select 'Clubs' from the menu, followed by 'find a club', to locate a hockey club near where you live. You might also be interested in finding out how else you could take part in a hockey match. There are plenty of opportunities for volunteers. If this interests you, choose 'Volunteering' from the main menu to find out more. Alternatively, if you are interested in umpiring, select the 'Umpiring' button to find out what you need to do to become an umpire, including the Young Umpire Award for 8–13 year olds and the Foundation Umpire Award for those who are 13 years plus.

If it is hockey in Ireland that you would like to gain information on, go to www.hockey.ie and select 'Kids and Development' to find out how you can become involved in hockey in Ireland and Northern Ireland. Hockey in Northern Ireland is run by the Ulster branch of the Irish Hockey Association. They can be contacted at:

Hockey Office
House of Sport
Upper Malone Road
Belfast BT9 5LA
Tel: 028-9038 3826.

www.scottish-hockey.org.uk offers options for finding a club in Scotland, as well as camps to improve your hockey skills. Select 'Youth' from the main menu to find out more. This link will also enable you to find out more about the Youth Umpire Award in Scotland.

If you are based in Wales and want to learn more about how to get involved in hockey, go to www.welsh-hockey.co.uk and click on the 'About' page. Select the icon allowing you to browse Welsh hockey clubs by region to find a club near you, or contact the development officer for further help. Their details may be found by selecting 'Development' from the main menu.

Top tip: Enjoy yourself. Hockey is about having fun, keeping fit, respecting the game and learning new skills.

© Alan Edwards

understanding hockey

Glossary

Advantage
After an infringement, the umpire may allow play to continue, rather than stop play. The umpire will usually do this if stopping play would disadvantage the infringed team.

Aerial ball
A ball that has been intentionally raised with a flick or a scoop so that it travels a long distance. When an aerial ball comes back to earth, the player nearest to where it lands must play it without any interference from other players, until it has been controlled and grounded.

Backline
The lines marking the two shortest sides of the rectangular pitch.

Blade
Another name for the flat face of a hockey stick.

Bully
A method of restarting a match when it has been stopped because of unforeseen circumstances, where both teams have infringed simultaneously or where an accident has occurred but no rule has been infringed upon.

Centre pass
The method for starting and restarting the game after half-time.

Flick
A means of passing the ball so it is pushed with the stick and raised from the ground.

Formation
The way the players are positioned around the pitch.

Goal line
The backline between the goalposts.

Jab
A type of tackle where the player pokes the ball away from the attacker and out of her possession.

Penalty flick
Another name for a penalty stroke.

Push
A method of passing the ball, which uses a quick wrist action with no backswing. The ball is pushed and directed along the ground. When the push occurs, both the ball and the head of the stick are on the ground.

Raised ball
A ball that is airborne. If a ball is raised into the air as a result of a hit, the player has infringed upon the rules. Players, with the exception of the goalkeeper, should not deflect or hit a raised ball. It should be controlled and grounded.

Reverse stick
When a player turns his stick so that the blade points right, allowing the player to move the ball to the right.

Scoop
A method of making the ball airborne. The head of the stick is placed under the ball and then the player makes a lifting movement.

Short corner
Another name for a penalty corner.

Toe
Another name for the stick head.

Answers

Chapter 5

B i   False

   ii   True

   iii False

   iv   True

   v   False

   vi   True

   vii False

   viii False

Chapter 6

A i A bully is being taken.

   ii The bully is a set piece used to restart play in the event of an unforeseen occurrence for which no team is responsible, an accident where no one infringed the rules or an event where both teams infringed upon the rules simultaneously.

B i   A, B and C are in play. D is out of play.

   ii A hit-out

   iii c

   iv 5 m

Chapter 8

A i   An obstruction

   ii 5 m distance

   iii Raised ball

   iv Advantage

   v Kick

Chapter 9

A Advantage. This is used when it would disadvantage the team that was infringed against if the game was halted.

B

Offence	Penalty
A player is in the midfield. He has barged into another player, preventing them from gaining possession of the ball.	A free hit.
A defending player has deliberately knocked the ball across the backline. The player is not the goalkeeper.	A penalty corner.
While waiting for a penalty corner to be taken, a defending player positioned behind the backline repeatedly moves into the circle. The umpire has already warned the player.	A temporary suspension and a penalty stroke can be awarded to the other side.
Before a penalty stroke has been taken, the goalkeeper moves his feet from the goal line.	A caution followed by a warning if it happens again. If the goalkeeper is not preventing a goal from being scored, then the penalty stroke should be retaken. If at any point the umpire feels that the goalkeeper has prevented a goal from being scored, she can award a penalty goal.

Bibliography

Chand, Dhyan (2006) In *Encyclopædia Britannica*. Retrieved 1 September 2006, from Encyclopædia Britannica Premium Service: http://www.britannica.com/eb/article-9002195

Howells, M.K. (1996) *The Romance of Hockey's History*. London: M.K. Howells. ISBN: 0-950-1997-1-0.

Nockolds, Jane (2004) *A Guide to Umpiring Hockey*. Milton Keynes: England Hockey. ISBN: 0-9541169-3-3.

Whitaker, David (1997) *The Hockey Workshop – A Complete Game Guide*. Marlborough: The Crowwood Press. ISBN: 1-85223-727-9.

Useful websites

www.bbc.co.uk

www.englandhockey.co.uk

www.eurohockey.org

www.fihockey.org

www.scottish-hockey.org.uk

www.welsh-hockey.co.uk

Index